MW01277146

PLEASE .

Name
_____

Address
_____

Apt. or Suite #
_____

City, State ZIP
_____

Phone
_____

Email
_____

You know who you are. But in case you become separated from your copy of **Nine Stupid Things People Do To Mess Up Their Resume**—which is also your **Career Information Manager and Interview Preparation Guide,** then maybe a really nice person will send it back if you fill in this information. **It surely would be a shame to lose all of this organized career data!**

The U. S. Mail doesn't charge very much to deliver this little book.

Nine Stupid Things People Do To Mess Up Their Resume

Angela K. Durden

Publisher Information:

WRITER for HIRE!

648 McKenzie Circle
Stockbridge, GA 30281
(770) 389-4321
(770) 506-4397 Fax
Angelawrtr4hre@msn.com
ISBN# 0-9701356-0-2
Library of Congress Catalog Card Number: 00-191138

*All your career information is now in one place. So no matter who prepares your resume—your mama, sister, friend, yourself, a local typesetter, or a professional resume preparer—**you** are prepared to sell **YOU**!*

Foreword

Marcia A. Champagne
Partner
Jordan & Champagne Inter Search Ltd.

I have seen thousands of all types of resumes during my twenty-plus years of executive search experience with KPMG-Peat Marwick, Booz Allen & Hamilton and with my own international search firm of Jordan & Champagne Inter Search Ltd. It is truly amazing what can be put together with very little (or too much) thought.

Creating a resume is one of the most fearful and trying tasks—whether you are just graduating from college or are a department head of a Fortune 500 company. This is an introspective exercise most people try to avoid at all cost.

Over my career, I have been asked by hundreds of persons to prepare their resume for them. I truly believe doing it would be a disservice and I tell them so. Going through this exercise of writing your own resume forces a person to look at who they are, their strengths and weaknesses and the direction they want their future to take.

A poorly presented resume can do a lot of damage. Recruiters skim resumes looking for key words. They do not have time to sift through reams of paper and crazy formats. If this process gets too confusing they disregard it and move on. Often a person tries to be cute or unique in an attempt to grab the readers attention. But in most cases it will backfire. Some of my most memorable faux pas are the following:

- An 8"x10" photo of a family portrait with a cover letter written by the family describing the multiple positive characteristics of their dad. The resume followed. In this situation, who needs to hear a comment from a six year old? The comment may be true but what has it to do with what he can do for a company? It went in the trash and the resume was never read.

- A bound four-plus page resume with the history of the person from womb to present. To a professional recruiter, this document represents a person who is in love with the recruiting process. They forget the purpose of the document. It is another expensive, creative masterpiece which either goes in your personal favorite file because you can't bear to throw out this treasure or in the trash.

- An eight-plus page resume with the last four pages of the document listing all patents, awards, articles, organizations, references, books written, etc. A real sign of a egotist. This is an early sign of a non-team player and red flags start flying. You have to include the me stuff, but it must be balanced with what has been accomplished or contributed in your ***previous positions on the company's behalf***. It may not go in the trash, but in a pile of if and when's.

There may be a time and a place for all of that information, but the resume is not it. In any case, the job seeker did not present himself in such a way as to secure an interview.

A person must prepare this very personal of documents in a way that is simple for, and easy on the eyes of, the reader, which in most cases is a professional recruiter. Often companies hire anonymous mailing centers to collect and screen resumes. These services are given key words in order to weed out candidates and then give the resume a quick (often 30 seconds or less) review.

A resume needs to be honest and thoughtful. You are who you are and know what you know....*be proud of it.* Yes, it is much more difficult to condense the information to fit one page than it is to write ten pages. But don't be mistaken—in this area, short and less complicated will get much better results.

After reading *Nine Stupid Things People Do To Mess Up Their Resume*, I believe it to be the best resource I have seen to assist anyone through this fearful task of resume writing. It gives the resume writer direction on how to present themselves in the clearest most distinct manner. Avoiding these nine pit falls will put you light years ahead in preparing an effective resume.

But, even more important, the additional sections in the book are designed to help you reflect on yourself, preparing you for that very important event—*the interview.* Going through these simple and fun areas in the book gently forces you to look at *you* and only you. There are no right or wrong answers; instead it is the beginning of your shedding light on the areas that make you unique and most valuable to a future employer.

Interviews themselves are very interesting. Over the years I have developed favorite interview questions. My most favorite is "Describe yourself using three adjectives." I only wish I had a recording of the responses and reactions to this simple question. I remember one very senior executive looking at me and pondering the request for what seemed like five minutes. He then said, "I CAN'T." Another executive started to pontificate on his virtue. Stopping him midstream, I said, "Just *three* adjectives". He froze. It took him an uncomfortable period to regroup and move on. Also, candidates have become anxious because they have simply forgotten what an adjective is!

Seeking a new position is the most important assignment one can do because it assures future prosperity. With the help of *Nine Stupid Things People Do To Mess Up Their Resume*, this task can now be accomplished with more ease and, very importantly, success!

Start today and have fun!

PREFACE

"Doing business without advertising is like winking at a girl in the dark. YOU know what you are doing, but NOBODY else does."

STEUART HENDERSON BRITT,
New York Herald Tribune, October 30, 1956

Is your resume winking in the dark? A resume is an advertisement designed to open the door to an interview. For as long as I have been preparing resumes, each appointment almost always follows the same pattern. The Job Seeker does not:

1. Have his entire work history details
2. Remember key information.
3. Know what an employer wants and needs.

Ladies and gentlemen. You cannot effectively advertise what you don't know. You also cannot effectively advertise if you know nothing about the possible buyer. Therefore, this book. It is not a book full of OPR (Other People's Resumes). You are looking for a job for YOU, not someone else.

It is a book full of timeless (and time-saving) hints, tips, and just plain common-sense that will help you put together your career information for greatest impact. It is a book that will enable you to manage your career information by giving you ONE place to keep ALL pertinent job related information.

It is a book that will allow you to quickly review your history just before that crucial interview. It is a book that you can take with you when filling out all those pesky (but necessary) employment applications. (That's right. No more forgetting an important chunk of information. It's all here!)

It is a book that will be your companion for many, many years to come. Enjoy.

Table of Contents

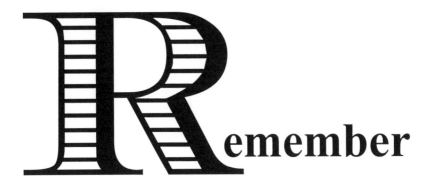

Remember

Your resume is your advertisement and an advertisement tells a story in such a way that the person seeing it will turn into a buyer.

What do you want your resume to tell about you?
You want it to tell not only what you CAN do,
but also how you have IMPROVED over the years.

You are not content with the status quo, no sir. You constantly strive to learn and improve your skills. You will bring to that business an eagerness to get the job done, improve productivity and make customers happy, thereby contributing to the financial health and longevity of the business.

If a business is being smart, they will hire you!

Now get busy and SELL yourself!

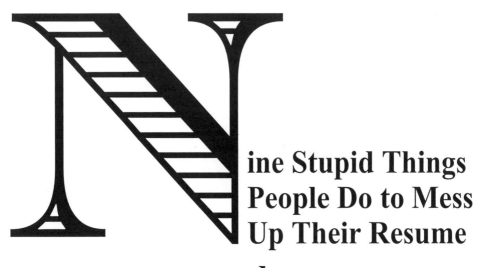

Nine Stupid Things People Do to Mess Up Their Resume

and

16 Ways You Can Avoid the Traps!

1 Stupid Spelling & Word Usage

It has been reported that corporate employment departments receive as many as 50,000 resumes per year; yet they hire only 200 to 300. Each resume is given a quick 30-second review. On which resumes do you think they will spend more time? That's right, those that are easily read, user friendly, and very, very clear.

Do not rely solely on your word processor's spell checker. While the words may be **spelled correctly,** it doesn't mean it is the word you want. Sometimes just **simple typos are real words** and your spell checker does not check for proper usage. Time to dust off Webster's! After all, you don't want your resume to look like a *ruff draught*, do you!

Please, I beg, **do not use a grammar check program** either. One fellow typed in the Gettysburg Address and used all the suggestions the grammar check program made. If Lincoln had given this speech the crowd would have turned on him. Use your common sense and ask someone else if they understand everything you wrote.

HINT!

To thoroughly spell check read aloud your resume to a friend who also has a copy. If you cannot do that, take a ruler (or other straight edge) and lay it under the first line of type. This will focus your eye on specific words and will not allow the eye to jump around in a random manner.

It may take a little bit of extra time, but it is well worth it.

 # Stupid Font Usage

Thousands of fonts exist and more are being created every day. But most of these are literally just variations on a theme. A designer may like the look of Times New Roman, but wants to make the capital letters just a little bit taller. He then calls it Smithfield (because his name is Smith and he lives near a field). Then he sells it and the consumer now has another font that they think is radically different.

Because of the availability of computers with word processing programs and the abundance of thousands of typefaces or fonts, some people get the idea they must use a little bit of everything in every document they create.

please, that couldn't be **FURTHER** from the truth!

Please limit the typefaces to a maximum of two. More than two and you run the risk of making the reader's eyes strain so hard to get the information they just throw away your resume in frustration.

HINT!

While the Pallatino font may be the most legible for a computer to scan, usually the two fonts below are native to most computer systems, thus readily available and perfectly acceptable. If you use either one or the other of the following fonts you will be fine.

Times New Roman
Times New Roman Bold
Times New Roman Italic
Times New Roman Italic Bold

and

Arial
Arial Bold
Arial Italic
Arial Italic Bold

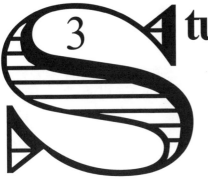tupid Layouts

HAVE YOU EVER SEEN SOMETHING TYPED IN ALL CAPITALS AND WITH NO TABS OR OTHER PUNCTUATION AND EVERYTHING JUST SORT OF ALL FLOWS TOGETHER BECAUSE THE PERSON WHO IS WRITING DOESN'T WANT TO TAKE THE TIME TO LEARN HOW TO USE THE WORD PROCESSOR AND SO JUST FIGURES IF THE WORDS ARE THERE THEN THE PERSON READING THE RESUME CAN JUST READ IT AND HIRE HIM ON THE SPOT BECAUSE HE IS SUCH A GENIUS? WELL THIS PERSON WILL MORE THAN LIKELY NOT GET HIRED.

There is a reason tabs and bullets exist. They help to offset information for the purpose of drawing attention to it. A sample resume showing font and tab usage is at the back of the book.

- Of course, the use of each must be judicious. **Too many bullets and nothing will stand out as special.** Too
- many tabs and information will not flow across the page. Bullets hugely sized in relation to the text (I know, you already
- see the big dots at left) detracts from the information.

HINT!

Use too many of these dots • and the reader will think they are playing connect the dots.

 4 Stupid Length

Less is more. Correctly written and formatted, all information should easily fit on one page. If information is split between two pages and one is misplaced, the headhunter will not have the whole story. You can bank on this: *they will not spend any time looking for it.*

I once met a man whose resume was **five pages long**. He asked me to read it and give my opinion. He was very proud of his resume and it is always hard to give bad news to someone who does not expect it.

The career path involved an extremely technical and very specialized set of skills. I read the resume and found that most of the **information was redundant**. He had performed the same job for five different employers. The following conversation ensued:

Question: Why have you written the same information over and over?

Answer: Because I have done all of this for all of them.

Question: Are you trying to get a job doing the same thing?

Answer: Yes.

Question: Have the companies to whom you are applying been in this business a long time?

Answer: Yes.

Question: So they are aware of what is involved in the job you want?

Answer: Yes.

Question: Then why do you have to tell them five times?

Answer: He got mad.

The conversation ended there. Hey, if you don't want to know, don't ask!

HINT!
Only tell enough information to leave them wanting more!

HINT!

A resume should only be one page. If you truly need two, then divide the information like this:

Page 1:

1. Name, address, and other contact information.
2. Objective, if you have one.
3. Dates of employment, employer, job title, and brief summation of accomplishments.
4. Skills summary.
5. Work ethic summary (see **Describe Yourself** section).
6. Education.

Page 2:

1. Name, address, and other contact information.
2. Employer, job title, and **detailed** job description, functions, and accomplishments.

Using this method you will have enough information on both pages so that, should one become separated from the other (and it happens!) the employer still knows who you are and what you can do for them.

# tupid Content

Remember your audience. They do not know you. But they want to know you because you may be THE one their company is looking for. Your resume is your advertisement. An advertisement tells *Who* you are; *What* you have done; *When* and *Where* you did it; *How* to get in touch with you; and *Why* you will be good for a company.

I am not lying here, okay? People really do forget to put in their **current address and phone number**.

They also list **every job** they have ever had since they began babysitting at age twelve. They list hobbies, children, marriages, sicknesses, why they moved, and why they left a job. They send family pictures. The resume reader knows the entire life history of the applicant. The resume reader doesn't care about your life history. He just wants to know the facts about your work.

Mean what you say and **say what you mean**. A good test of whether or not you are being clear is to say the words out loud and then pretend the person you are talking to does not understand and asks for an explanation. You simply will not be able to repeat yourself. *You must use different words.*

If you cannot use different words to explain it to the satisfaction of another, then you are not clear about what you do and know. If you **cannot explain it**, then the thinking goes, **you must not really know it.** Guess who won't be hired?

HINT!

Condensing your explanation and putting it on paper helps to clarify what you mean. Let someone else read it. Do they have questions?

HINT!

If you have held many jobs, don't worry about it. Simply list those jobs held during the past ten years. If two jobs were held concurrently and you were at one only a short time, you may choose to leave it out. If you held any job for less than two months, again you may choose to leave it out.

However, **any skills learned on any job can still be listed**. A resume is not your life history; it should show your stability and job skills.

6 Stupid Career Objectives

Have you ever seen a television commercial that was very memorable but you couldn't remember what product was being sold? That is a commercial that is not sure of what it wants to do. Make sure the resume reader knows what you want and can do for them.

Favorite Career Objective: To work for a successful company that values its employees and to be rewarded with promotion.

Next Favorite Objective: To use my abilities and talents to further the goals of your company.

No kidding? Really?!? Can anybody get any more vague, uninspiring, and boring? Well, they certainly do keep trying. These two objectives mentioned above should be a **given** for any employee. We know people who really don't want to work; they just want to be paid to look busy. I have heard it said these folks should apply to their local, state, and federal government and stay out of private industry.

Ask and answer the following questions before you send out that next resume.

1. What kind of job would you like to have? (Can't make a wish come true until you know what it is.)

_____

_____

_____

2. What does the job look like that you want to have five years from now?

_____

_____

_____

3. Write a specific job title or brief simple phrase describing the type of work or challenge you are seeking.

_____

_____

_____

4. What most interests you professionally?

_____

_____

_____

5. What are your professional long range goals?

_____

_____

_____

6. What are your short range goals?

_____

_____

_____

HINT!

In order to answer the professional long range goal question, you may need to ask yourself what your personal long range goals are. Often to reach one or the other a sacrifice must be made. Which are you willing to sacrifice in order to get the other?

HINT!

*If you are unsure for what you are looking, or are unclear as to what you want to do, then for goodness sake, do not put in a vague objective. **There is no law that says a resume must have an objective.***

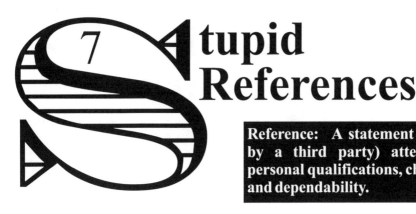 7 tupid References

> **Reference: A statement (usually by a third party) attesting to personal qualifications, character, and dependability.**

Let me state this in as clear a manner as possible:

Do NOT List References!

Yes, you read correctly. I know. I know. Everyone has been taught to either list references directly on the resume or make a note at the bottom: *References Supplied Upon Request.*

Why is that a stupid thing to do? Two reasons. *One:* listing all these people takes up valuable space you can use to sell yourself. Why clutter your advertisement?

Two: Employers know if you do not give references when they ask, you won't be in the running anyway. Why state the obvious?

HINT!

However, there is something completely permissible you can do. In a folder kept separate from your resume, have a prepared **Reference Sheet** of those friends, relatives, and past business associates who can vouch for your character. Should an interviewer decide you are a particularly hot prospect and want to start checking on you right away, you may hand them this separate sheet.

In fact, this shows forethought, preparation, and planning. They will think you have it on the ball!

8 Stupid Salary History

Headhunters uniformly pigeonhole applicants by their salary history. You won't even get an audience if the job pays $130,000 and you are making $80,000.

PRO

The employer may have a salary cap which would put you in the poor house. Obviously, there will not be a fit, so why should either of you waste your time?

CON

The employer may like what he sees. But because your salary requirements are higher than he is allowed to go, he thinks you are completely and totally out of his ballpark. No salary history will allow an opportunity to discuss options in pay, benefits, and other perks.

Hey, act like the folks you read about in the *Forbes* and *Inc*. magazines. Keep your options open and realize there are other things that can contribute to a healthy bottom line other than a certain dollar figure on your paycheck.

HINT!

Make a list of everything you spend money on. Be ruthless! Whether you spend it on an ice cream cone (at $2.00 a cone) or toilet paper, the money is gone. Now, take a look at that list. Ask yourself if there are other ways you can get the same thing by trading for it in your new job.

For instance: *Does that job you are interested in sound really good but the pay just won't cover your after school child care costs? Then tell them you will take the pay they offer **IF** they will allow you to leave work in time to be home when your child arrives from school. You and your child will benefit from seeing each other more each day and the employer will have a happy employee who will stay around a good long time. Besides, you will miss rush hour traffic!*

tupid Lies

Lie: A false statement or piece of information *deliberately* presented as being true to mislead or deceive in order to get what you want.

HINT!

Every business has customers. These customers rely on the expertise, knowledge, and abilities of the business's employees to provide them with what they are purchasing. They rely on their being able to tell them how to use the product. They rely on having their product serviced so that it works a while longer.

But let's say a business has hired someone who has deceived them. He could talk the talk but he hardly knew where the dipstick was. Do you really want him working on YOUR car? Of course not! So, please, do not fudge the facts. You may get away with it for a short while, but in the end, the customer gets a bad impression of the business; the business loses money and must shut down. Either way, you have to look for another job. Bummer.

Tell one lie and more lies will need to be told to cover it up. As one wise man once said, "a liar should have a good memory". As another said, "tell the truth and you can have a bad memory". You have probably heard people who brag of their sharp business practices. These very often are lies and they cut both ways. Remember, a lie is nothing but a false statement (with maybe a little bit of truth) intended to get someone else to do their bidding. Go ahead. Buy a lemon of a car. Buy the horribly written computer program. Employ an unqualified person. Who will it hurt?

Please, do not lie about any college education. These claims are ALWAYS confirmed with the college, so you better have the degree you say you do.

End of
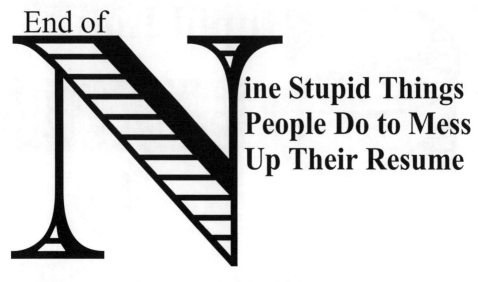
ine Stupid Things People Do to Mess Up Their Resume

Now on to Selling YOU!

In this section you will find a step-by-step guide to managing your career information. Forget the other books that simply copy other people's resumes and then tell you to adapt them for your own use.

Here you will learn the nitty-gritty of YOUR career, YOUR abilities and qualifications, YOUR strengths and weaknesses. You will learn what you think about yourself and what others think, too. Ignore the popular admonition and write in this book. Go ahead. It is allowed. Then please, write and tell me what you think. (Was it helpful? Could it be improved? Did you have any suggestions?) Did you recommend it? I would love to hear from you.

WRITER for HIRE!
648 McKenzie Circle
Stockbridge, Georgia 30281
Angelawrtr4hre@msn.com

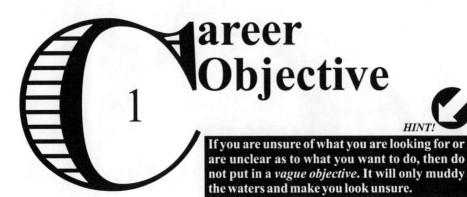

Career Objective

1

HINT!

If you are unsure of what you are looking for or are unclear as to what you want to do, then do not put in a *vague objective*. It will only muddy the waters and make you look unsure.

1. What kind of job would you like to have? *(Can't make a wish come true until you know what it is!)*

   _____

   _____

2. What does the job look like that you want to have five years from now?

   _____

   _____

3. Write a specific job title or brief simple phrase describing the type of work you are seeking.

   _____

   _____

4. What most interests you professionally?

   _____

   _____

5. What are your long range professional goals ?

   _____

   _____

6. What are your long range personal goals?

   _____

   _____

7. What are your short range professional goals ?

   _____

   _____

8. What are your short range personal goals?

   _____

   _____

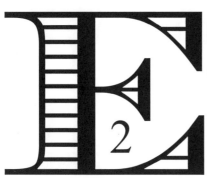 **ducation**
(Formal)

HINT!

The dates listed here are for YOUR information and may or may not be included on a resume. Written dates allow someone to put an age on you that could hamper your possibilities. Yes, yes. I know it is against the law to discriminate on the basis of age, but you and I both know it happens. On the other hand, if you do not list the dates so the degree can be confirmed then you are out of the running anyway.

Diploma/Degree Obtained	Course of Study	School Name	Graduation Year

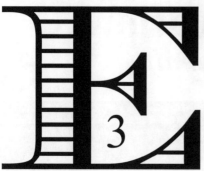

Education
(Other)

HINT!
List any management or other
training seminars, classes, etc.

Course of Study	School Name	Year

Skills Summary

4

HINT!

This section will cover computer and other skills including office procedures. You will be surprised how much you really know!

Software Applications:
- [ ] Word Processing
- [ ] Graphics
- [ ] Online Research
- [ ] Database
- [ ] Web Page Design
- [ ] Spreadsheet
- [ ] Accounting
- [ ] E-mail
- [ ] Desktop Publishing
- [ ] Presentation Software

Operating Systems:
- [ ] DOS ___.x
- [ ] UNIX
- [ ] Networks
- [ ] MacIntosh
- [ ] LAN's
- [ ] Windows 3.x
- [ ] Windows 9x
- [ ] Programming
- [ ] Other

Hardware Systems:
- [ ] Setting Up
- [ ] Troubleshooting
- [ ] Upgrading

Describe Your Level of Knowledge:
(Remember, For Your Eyes Only!)
- [ ] How do I turn it on?
- [ ] Right click? Is there a wrong click?
- [ ] I can write a letter and, on a good day, get it to print.
- [ ] Everybody in the office comes to me for help.
- [ ] Move over! Total Techno-Nerd is here!

Office Machines:
- [ ] Adding Machine
- [ ] Dot Matrix Printer
- [ ] Laser Printer
- [ ] Ink Jet Printer
- [ ] Fax
- [ ] Copier
- [ ] Scanner
- [ ] Typewriter
  (Yes, these are still used!)

Office Procedures:
- [ ] Excellent phone manners and voice
- [ ] Take thorough messages and confirm delivery

- [ ] Research customer billing inquiries
- [ ] Research vendor billings
- [ ] Filing
- [ ] Purchase Orders
- [ ] Interviewing Vendors
- [ ] Recognizing Efficient Methods
- [ ] Implementing Efficient Methods
- [ ] Interdepartmental Liaison
- [ ] General Bookkeeping
- [ ] Writing Employee Manuals

HINT!

See next page for more detailed skills.

☐ **Insurance:** *Health; Worker's Comp; Dental*

☐ **Scheduling:** *Employees; Job crews*

☐ **Accounts Receivables:** *Invoicing, Posting payments, Preparing and sending payments*

☐ **Accounts Payable:** *Correctly paying vendors, Writing checks, Preparing bank deposits.*

☐ **Payroll:** *Time tracking, Data entry, New Employee set up, W-2's, W-4's, G-4's, 1099's, Extra withholding, Issuing checks.*

☐ **Paying Taxes:** *FUTA, SUTA, EFTPS, Direct Federal Tax Deposits.*

☐ **Supervisory Skills:** *Delegation; Recognition of employee limits; Decision making processes; Accountable for own decisions and actions; Making presentations; Teaching; Training; Mediating; Admitting mistakes; Apologizing; Helping others to be able to apologize; Helping others to be able to admit mistakes.*

☐ **Project Manager:** *Coming up with the idea; Breaking it down into smaller steps; Choosing a team with which to work; Implementing each step; Gathering materials; Presenting finished project.*

OTHER STUFF:

_____

Didn't know you knew so much, did you?

Obviously, this list does not cover every single thing a person can do on a job. But if you feel I have left out something very important or think the list can be improved in any manner, then please email your suggestions and thoughts to **Angelawrtr4hre@msn.com**. We just may incorporate them in the next edition.

Languages

5

I fluently speak:

_____

_____

_____

I fluently read:

_____

_____

_____

I fluently write:

_____

_____

_____

I have a working knowledge of:

_____

_____

_____

6 Awards, Honors, Clubs, & Teams

HINT!

Teams and clubs may show abilities to work productively with a group. Honors and awards speak loudly and clearly of your abilities. While you may not want to put this on your resume, you may begin to see a pattern of accomplishment and abilities that can be neatly translated to the work place.

Name or describe any of the above and the year you did each. Make a note of any written evaluations received.

Team, Club, Honor, or Award	Year	Notes on activities with Team or Club and What the Award and Honor was for

Licenses and Certificates

7

HINT!

If the license or certificate does not apply to the particular position you are currently seeking but feel in the future it may come in handy for this employer, *do not hesitate to point this out at the time of the interview,* not on the resume. Do put it on the resume if it will have a direct bearing on whether or not you will qualify for the job.

List licenses or certificates you hold whether or not they are pertinent to the job you are seeking and the year you obtained each.

License or Certificate Name	Year Obtained

Qualification #1

8a

HINT!

> Use concrete examples such as:
>
> Researched and interviewed seven potential vendors for XYZ, Inc.'s worker's comp insurance needs. When all the information was in, the vendor we chose saved the company $XXXX per year over our then current vendor.
> or
> After my company began using the system I designed, we saved $XXXX.
> or
> What formerly took three weeks now takes only one week because of the efficient production method I designed.

Clearly describe your *MOST* valuable work related achievement.

Qualification #2

8b

HINT!

Include points that will help sell you to an employer.
Example: The first thing I want someone to
remember about me is _____.

or

_____ inspires and motivates me to do my
best.

or

To me, success means _____.

*Remember, a resume is your advertisement!
Sell! Sell! Sell!*

**Clearly describe another
of your valuable work
related traits.**

8c Qualification #3

HINT!

Clearly describe another of your valuable work related traits.

Use another concrete example. Use your sentences on pages 44-46 to find other examples.

Describe Yourself

9a

HINT!

A resume needs to concentrate on the good stuff! Put in today's date and in one year describe yourself again on the next page. Be sure to notice your many improvements.

Remember, this list of adjectives is for your eyes only. Don't be shy. You will notice only positive traits are listed. That is because most of us usually have no trouble underestimating ourselves. Check those words that best describe your work ethic, style, and personality.

Date:

❑ Reverent	❑ Tolerant	❑ Positive	❑ Dutiful
❑ Versatile	❑ Involved	❑ Pleasant	❑ Giving
❑ Agreeable	❑ Stable	❑ Helpful	❑ Studious
❑ Effective	❑ Talented	❑ Proud	❑ Exact
❑ Selfless	❑ Eager	❑ Leader	❑ Skillful
❑ Content	❑ Alert	❑ Competent	❑ Supportive
❑ Discreet	❑ Generous	❑ Organized	❑ Approachable
❑ Accurate	❑ Kind	❑ Sympathetic	❑ Conformist
❑ Capable	❑ Productive	❑ Progressive	❑ Traditional
❑ Willing	❑ Positive	❑ Fervent	❑ Enterprising
❑ Detail-Oriented	❑ Able	❑ Funny	❑ Disciplined
❑ Meticulous	❑ Motivated	❑ Honest	❑ Receptive
❑ Open-Minded	❑ Quality-Minded	❑ Patient	❑ Particular
❑ Mannerly	❑ Courteous	❑ Participator	❑ Daring
❑ Constant	❑ Respectful	❑ Good-Natured	❑ Prompt
❑ Tactful	❑ Responsible	❑ Diplomatic	❑ Loyal
❑ Dignified	❑ Dynamic	❑ Zealous	❑ Busy
❑ Faithful	❑ Demanding	❑ Adaptable	❑ Handy
❑ Balanced	❑ Excited	❑ Reputable	❑ Ethical
❑ Energetic	❑ Prepared	❑ Observant	❑ Sharp
❑ Peaceful	❑ Thorough	❑ Sensitive	❑ Quick

Describe Yourself
9b

Remember, this list of adjectives is for your eyes only. Don't be shy. You will notice only positive traits are listed. That is because most of us usually have no trouble underestimating ourselves. Check those words that best describe your work ethic, style, and personality.

HINT!

A resume needs to concentrate on the good stuff! Well? Have you grown in value to your employer? Bet you have! Now, sell it, baby!

Date:

❏ Reverent	❏ Tolerant	❏ Positive	❏ Dutiful
❏ Versatile	❏ Involved	❏ Pleasant	❏ Giving
❏ Agreeable	❏ Stable	❏ Helpful	❏ Studious
❏ Effective	❏ Talented	❏ Proud	❏ Exact
❏ Selfless	❏ Eager	❏ Leader	❏ Skillful
❏ Content	❏ Alert	❏ Competent	❏ Supportive
❏ Discreet	❏ Generous	❏ Organized	❏ Approachable
❏ Accurate	❏ Kind	❏ Sympathetic	❏ Conformist
❏ Capable	❏ Productive	❏ Progressive	❏ Traditional
❏ Willing	❏ Positive	❏ Fervent	❏ Enterprising
❏ Detail-Oriented	❏ Able	❏ Funny	❏ Disciplined
❏ Meticulous	❏ Motivated	❏ Honest	❏ Receptive
❏ Open-Minded	❏ Quality-Minded	❏ Patient	❏ Particular
❏ Mannerly	❏ Courteous	❏ Participator	❏ Daring
❏ Constant	❏ Respectful	❏ Good-Natured	❏ Prompt
❏ Tactful	❏ Responsible	❏ Diplomatic	❏ Loyal
❏ Dignified	❏ Dynamic	❏ Zealous	❏ Busy
❏ Faithful	❏ Demanding	❏ Adaptable	❏ Handy
❏ Balanced	❏ Excited	❏ Reputable	❏ Ethical
❏ Energetic	❏ Prepared	❏ Observant	❏ Sharp
❏ Peaceful	❏ Thorough	❏ Sensitive	❏ Quick

Let a *FRIEND* Describe You

10a

HINT!

We often see things about others they don't see. So let someone fill out this for you. You just may be surprised what others see in you. It takes a lot of courage to ask for this kind of feedback. It also takes a lot of courage to give it honestly. Remember, if it isn't all that you hoped it would be, don't be mad at your friend. Forewarned is forearmed. Use this feedback to strengthen those areas.

See yourself through the eyes of your boss, friend, coworker, career counselor, professor, or teacher. **Let a friend check off those words that best describe what they think about your work ethic, style, and personality.**

❑ Reverent	❑ Tolerant	❑ Positive	❑ Dutiful
❑ Versatile	❑ Involved	❑ Pleasant	❑ Giving
❑ Agreeable	❑ Stable	❑ Helpful	❑ Studious
❑ Effective	❑ Talented	❑ Proud	❑ Exact
❑ Selfless	❑ Eager	❑ Leader	❑ Skillful
❑ Content	❑ Alert	❑ Competent	❑ Supportive
❑ Discreet	❑ Generous	❑ Organized	❑ Approachable
❑ Accurate	❑ Kind	❑ Sympathetic	❑ Conformist
❑ Capable	❑ Productive	❑ Progressive	❑ Traditional
❑ Willing	❑ Positive	❑ Fervent	❑ Enterprising
❑ Detail-Oriented	❑ Able	❑ Funny	❑ Disciplined
❑ Meticulous	❑ Motivated	❑ Honest	❑ Receptive
❑ Open-Minded	❑ Quality-Minded	❑ Patient	❑ Particular
❑ Mannerly	❑ Courteous	❑ Participator	❑ Daring
❑ Constant	❑ Respectful	❑ Good-Natured	❑ Prompt
❑ Tactful	❑ Responsible	❑ Diplomatic	❑ Loyal
❑ Dignified	❑ Dynamic	❑ Zealous	❑ Busy
❑ Faithful	❑ Demanding	❑ Adaptable	❑ Handy
❑ Balanced	❑ Excited	❑ Reputable	❑ Ethical
❑ Energetic	❑ Prepared	❑ Observant	❑ Sharp
❑ Peaceful	❑ Thorough	❑ Sensitive	❑ Quick

Let a *Coworker* Describe You

10b

HINT!

We often see things about others they don't see. So let someone fill out this for you. You just may be surprised what others see in you. It takes a lot of courage to ask for this kind of feedback. It also takes a lot of courage to give it honestly. Remember, if it isn't all that you hoped it would be, don't be mad at your coworker. Forewarned is forearmed. Use this feedback to strengthen those areas.

Let a coworker check off those words that best describe what they think about your work ethic, style, and personality.

❑ Reverent	❑ Tolerant	❑ Positive	❑ Dutiful
❑ Versatile	❑ Involved	❑ Pleasant	❑ Giving
❑ Agreeable	❑ Stable	❑ Helpful	❑ Studious
❑ Effective	❑ Talented	❑ Proud	❑ Exact
❑ Selfless	❑ Eager	❑ Leader	❑ Skillful
❑ Content	❑ Alert	❑ Competent	❑ Supportive
❑ Discreet	❑ Generous	❑ Organized	❑ Approachable
❑ Accurate	❑ Kind	❑ Sympathetic	❑ Conformist
❑ Capable	❑ Productive	❑ Progressive	❑ Traditional
❑ Willing	❑ Positive	❑ Fervent	❑ Enterprising
❑ Detail-Oriented	❑ Able	❑ Funny	❑ Disciplined
❑ Meticulous	❑ Motivated	❑ Honest	❑ Receptive
❑ Open-Minded	❑ Quality-Minded	❑ Patient	❑ Particular
❑ Mannerly	❑ Courteous	❑ Participator	❑ Daring
❑ Constant	❑ Respectful	❑ Good-Natured	❑ Prompt
❑ Tactful	❑ Responsible	❑ Diplomatic	❑ Loyal
❑ Dignified	❑ Dynamic	❑ Zealous	❑ Busy
❑ Faithful	❑ Demanding	❑ Adaptable	❑ Handy
❑ Balanced	❑ Excited	❑ Reputable	❑ Ethical
❑ Energetic	❑ Prepared	❑ Observant	❑ Sharp
❑ Peaceful	❑ Thorough	❑ Sensitive	❑ Quick

Let a *RELATIVE* Describe You

10c

HINT!

We often see things about others they don't see. So let someone fill out this for you. You just may be surprised what others see in you. It takes a lot of courage to ask for this kind of feedback. It also takes a lot of courage to give it honestly. Remember, if it isn't all that you hoped it would be, don't be mad at your relative. Forewarned is forearmed. Use this feedback to strengthen those areas.

Let a relative check off those words that best describe what they think about your work ethic, style, and personality.

☐ Reverent	☐ Tolerant	☐ Positive	☐ Dutiful
☐ Versatile	☐ Involved	☐ Pleasant	☐ Giving
☐ Agreeable	☐ Stable	☐ Helpful	☐ Studious
☐ Effective	☐ Talented	☐ Proud	☐ Exact
☐ Selfless	☐ Eager	☐ Leader	☐ Skillful
☐ Content	☐ Alert	☐ Competent	☐ Supportive
☐ Discreet	☐ Generous	☐ Organized	☐ Approachable
☐ Accurate	☐ Kind	☐ Sympathetic	☐ Conformist
☐ Capable	☐ Productive	☐ Progressive	☐ Traditional
☐ Willing	☐ Positive	☐ Fervent	☐ Enterprising
☐ Detail-Oriented	☐ Able	☐ Funny	☐ Disciplined
☐ Meticulous	☐ Motivated	☐ Honest	☐ Receptive
☐ Open-Minded	☐ Quality-Minded	☐ Patient	☐ Particular
☐ Mannerly	☐ Courteous	☐ Participator	☐ Daring
☐ Constant	☐ Respectful	☐ Good-Natured	☐ Prompt
☐ Tactful	☐ Responsible	☐ Diplomatic	☐ Loyal
☐ Dignified	☐ Dynamic	☐ Zealous	☐ Busy
☐ Faithful	☐ Demanding	☐ Adaptable	☐ Handy
☐ Balanced	☐ Excited	☐ Reputable	☐ Ethical
☐ Energetic	☐ Prepared	☐ Observant	☐ Sharp
☐ Peaceful	☐ Thorough	☐ Sensitive	☐ Quick

Let *Someone Else* Describe You

10d

HINT!

We often see things about others they don't see. So, let someone fill out this for you. You just may be surprised what others see in you. It takes a lot of courage to ask for this kind of feedback. It also takes a lot of courage to give it honestly. Remember, if it isn't all that you hoped it would be, don't be mad at your friend. Forewarned is forearmed. Use this feedback to strengthen those areas.

Let someone else check off those words that best describe what they think about your work ethic, style, and personality. Now compare all your lists and see where everyone agrees. More than likely these are your strengths!

❑ Reverent	❑ Tolerant	❑ Positive	❑ Dutiful
❑ Versatile	❑ Involved	❑ Pleasant	❑ Giving
❑ Agreeable	❑ Stable	❑ Helpful	❑ Studious
❑ Effective	❑ Talented	❑ Proud	❑ Exact
❑ Selfless	❑ Eager	❑ Leader	❑ Skillful
❑ Content	❑ Alert	❑ Competent	❑ Supportive
❑ Discreet	❑ Generous	❑ Organized	❑ Approachable
❑ Accurate	❑ Kind	❑ Sympathetic	❑ Conformist
❑ Capable	❑ Productive	❑ Progressive	❑ Traditional
❑ Willing	❑ Positive	❑ Fervent	❑ Enterprising
❑ Detail-Oriented	❑ Able	❑ Funny	❑ Disciplined
❑ Meticulous	❑ Motivated	❑ Honest	❑ Receptive
❑ Open-Minded	❑ Quality-Minded	❑ Patient	❑ Particular
❑ Mannerly	❑ Courteous	❑ Participator	❑ Daring
❑ Constant	❑ Respectful	❑ Good-Natured	❑ Prompt
❑ Tactful	❑ Responsible	❑ Diplomatic	❑ Loyal
❑ Dignified	❑ Dynamic	❑ Zealous	❑ Busy
❑ Faithful	❑ Demanding	❑ Adaptable	❑ Handy
❑ Balanced	❑ Excited	❑ Reputable	❑ Ethical
❑ Energetic	❑ Prepared	❑ Observant	❑ Sharp
❑ Peaceful	❑ Thorough	❑ Sensitive	❑ Quick

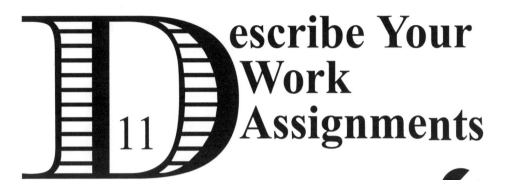

Describe Your Work Assignments

11

HINT!

A resume needs to show you can do more than just sit there.
The interviewer will want to know: Why you think you are capable of the position you are
interviewing for. How you justify your salary requirements.
And what you believe your last employer would say about you.

*These are action verbs that can describe **how** you did your work.*

❑ Accelerated	❑ Accomplished	❑ Achieved	❑ Adapted
❑ Administered	❑ Analyzed	❑ Approved	❑ Coordinated
❑ Conceived	❑ Conducted	❑ Completed	❑ Controlled
❑ Created	❑ Delegated	❑ Developed	❑ Demonstrated
❑ Designed	❑ Directed	❑ Effected	❑ Eliminated
❑ Established	❑ Evaluated	❑ Expanded	❑ Expedited
❑ Facilitated	❑ Found	❑ Generated	❑ Increased
❑ Influenced	❑ Implemented	❑ Initiated	❑ Instructed
❑ Interpreted	❑ Improved	❑ Launched	❑ Led
❑ Lectured	❑ Maintained	❑ Managed	❑ Originated
❑ Mastered	❑ Motivated	❑ Operated	❑ Planned
❑ Organized	❑ Participated	❑ Performed	❑ Proposed
❑ Pinpointed	❑ Programmed	❑ Programmed	❑ Reduced
❑ Proved	❑ Provided	❑ Finished	❑ Revised
❑ Recommended	❑ Reinforced	❑ Revamped	❑ Set Up
❑ Reviewed	❑ Scheduled	❑ Simplified	❑ Structured
❑ Solved	❑ Structured	❑ Solved	❑ Taught
❑ Streamlined	❑ Supervised	❑ Supported	❑ Won
❑ Trained	❑ Translated	❑ Utilized	❑ _____

11b *Take a little trip... Take a little trip... Take a little trip with me-eee!*

HINT!

Now that you know how you did it, tell me what you did it to. Write one sentence for each of the boxes you checked on the previous page. (Don't you just feel like you have taken a trip back in time to 5th grade and are having to write one sentence with each of your spelling words? And you thought you would NEVER need that skill in adult life!)

The resume reader will want to know what you did and how and why you did it. These facts will be used in your resume. Remember, all good advertising eventually has facts to back up the warm, fuzzy feelings. Motivate the reader of your resume to buy YOU!

PLEASE persevere. Believe me, the effort will be well worth it.

I Accelerated _____

I Administered _____

I Conceived _____

I Created _____

I Designed _____

I Established _____

I Facilitated _____

I Influenced _____

I Interpreted _____

I Lectured _____

I Mastered _____

I Organized _____

I Pinpointed _____

I Proved _____

I Recommended _____

I Reviewed _____

I Solved _____

I Streamlined _____

I Trained _____

I Accomplished _____

I Accomplished _____

I Analyzed _____

I Conducted _____

I Delegated _____

I Directed _____

I Evaluated _____

I Found _____

I Implemented _____

I Improved _____

I Maintained _____

I Motivated _____

I Participated _____

I Programmed _____

I Provided _____

I Reinforced _____

I Scheduled _____

I Structured _____

I Supervised _____

I Translated _____

I Achieved _____

I Approved _____

I Completed _____

I Developed _____

I Effected _____

I Expanded _____

I Generated _____

I Initiated _____

I Launched _____

I Managed _____

I Operated _____

I Programmed _____

I Finished _____

I Revamped _____

I Simplified _____

I Solved _____

I Supported _____

I Utilized _____

I Adapted _____

I Coordinated _____

I Controlled _____

I Demonstrated _____

I Eliminated _____

I Expedited _____

I Increased _____

I Instructed _____

I Led _____

I Originated _____

I Planned _____

I Proposed _____

I Reduced _____

I Revised _____

I Set Up _____

I Structured _____

I Taught _____

I Won _____

Go back and read everything you have done. Did you realize you had accomplished so much and were so valuable to an employer? You should now be much clearer on what you have to offer. Hey, you are learning to sell the *steak* and the *sizzle*!

HINT!

When writing your resume, do not use the title "I" anywhere in the resume (or at least as little as possible). If you accelerated a project say "Accelerated Project XYZ" NOT "I Accelerated Project XYZ". The word "I" will become very, very old after a while.

More Notes About Your Excellent Abilities

Career History 12

HINT!

How to Use This Section: Have you ever tried to fill out an application for employment or write your resume but couldn't remember everything you needed? The Career Information Manager & Interview Preparation Guide is great to take with you when filling out those exhausting applications.

While all your information may be on a computer diskette somewhere, it is extremely hard to read those disks while trying to fill out the application away from home. There is something to be said for low tech. Also, if you keep this in your purse or briefcase you can easily update it while the information about your current success is still fresh in your mind.

If you have been self-employed, list your clients!

Company Name	City, State

Ending Salary	Year Started & Ended

Position or Job Title

Reason For Leaving *(Do not put this information on your resume.)*

Did you do something for this company you are proud of? Write it here.
Refer to your Qualifications Section for possible references and ideas.

Company Name	City, State

Ending Salary   Year Started & Ended

Position or Job Title

Reason For Leaving *(Do not put this information on your resume.)*

Did you do something for this company you are proud of? Write it here.
Refer to your Qualifications Section for possible references and ideas.

Company Name

City, State

Ending Salary

Year Started & Ended

Position or Job Title

Reason For Leaving *(Do not put this information on your resume.)*

Did you do something for this company you are proud of? Write it here.
Refer to your Qualifications Section for possible references and ideas.

Company Name	City, State

Ending Salary   Year Started & Ended

Position or Job Title

Reason For Leaving *(Do not put this information on your resume.)*

Did you do something for this company you are proud of? Write it here.
Refer to your Qualifications Section for possible references and ideas.

Company Name	City, State

Ending Salary	Year Started & Ended

Position or Job Title

Reason For Leaving *(Do not put this information on your resume.)*

Did you do something for this company you are proud of? Write it here.
Refer to your Qualifications Section for possible references and ideas.

Company Name	City, State

Ending Salary   Year Started & Ended

Position or Job Title

Reason For Leaving *(Do not put this information on your resume.)*

Did you do something for this company you are proud of? Write it here.
Refer to your Qualifications Section for possible references and ideas.

Company Name   City, State

Ending Salary   Year Started & Ended

Position or Job Title

Reason For Leaving *(Do not put this information on your resume.)*

Did you do something for this company you are proud of? Write it here.
Refer to your Qualifications Section for possible references and ideas.

Company Name	City, State

Ending Salary	Year Started & Ended

Position or Job Title

Reason For Leaving *(Do not put this information on your resume.)*

Did you do something for this company you are proud of? Write it here.
Refer to your Qualifications Section for possible references and ideas.

Company Name	City, State

Ending Salary	Year Started & Ended

Position or Job Title

Reason For Leaving *(Do not put this information on your resume.)*

Did you do something for this company you are proud of? Write it here.
Refer to your Qualifications Section for possible references and ideas.

13 Volunteer Activities

HINT!

Volunteering for the PTA, Little League Fund Raisers, at a homeless shelter, answering phones at a Suicide or Runaway Hotline, with officials as a Victim's Advocate, even in your child's class, are opportunities for you to learn and hone skills that can be used in the PAID workplace. Don't discount your abilities.

I volunteered for:	What I did for them:

Interests

14

HINT!

These interests do not need to be listed on a resume, but you could be asked about them in an interview, so give it some thought ahead of time. Do not list things like partying or drag racing on the interstate with strangers. Do list things like restoring an old car, Bible study, crafts, reading business magazines, etc. You know, stuff that helps you be a better person and stimulates the mind ultimately bringing value to the employer and business.

Why Will I Be Good 15 for a Company?

This is often the hardest part to write or talk about. Why? Because employers do not want to hear only that you are a good person; they also want to know if you can work hard, steadily, and intelligently. Be precise when you tell them what you are able to do.

Describe your abilities and strengths. The word lists that you checked in the **Describe Yourself** and **Describe Your Work Assignments** sections, as well as the sentences you wrote with the action words, should give you more than enough examples of your abilities and accomplishments. If you are having a hard time with this, try this method: *role playing.*

First, pretend a friend has come to you for help with his resume. This friend, *of course*, has the same work history and personality as you. What would you tell your friend about himself? Would you simply rehash a litany of imperfections and mistakes? Of course not. You would make positive, truthful observations. You would remind him of the time he did that really neat thing that so impressed the boss because it saved the company a lot of time and money or further cemented a customer's loyalty.

Write these thoughts as they occur. Do not worry about how small the accomplishment looks in your eyes. Remember, pennies make dollars and a lot of smaller deeds consistently done add up to one great employee. Remove any repetitious information and put these in complete sentences. Check the spelling—*use a dictionary.* Put this information on pages 61 and 62.

Don't worry, you don't need to write a novel. Short sentences and simple statements are best.

HINT!

Think Like A Business Owner

A business owner wants to accomplish the most, at the highest quality, without spending one more dime than is necessary. This owner is going to be investing a lot of money in you. He will want to know: *why he should hire you; why you want this job; how you set priorities; will you be cooperative; can you overcome adversity and handle pressure; what you consider to be your biggest challenge to date; will you, can you, have you shown initiative; what is your idea of being successful; and what motivates you.*

Think about it now. Really. Right now, think about these things.

➤ Why should YOU be hired?
➤ Are you going to do the job asked of you and more?
➤ Are you going to have at heart the best interests of the company?
➤ Are you going to be more of a liability than an asset?
➤ Are you going to cost the company money by making rash decisions? Not showing up? Working at a snail's pace? Walking around constantly talking about non-job stuff? Forever talking on the phone to friends? Not putting forth effort to learn the job correctly? Insisting on your way when another is best?
➤ Will you always want the company to give you something for nothing?
➤ Will you ignore customers?
➤ Will you treat customers as if they are intruding on your personal time?

All of these are legitimate concerns. Let's face it. Haven't we all met people with these attitudes and didn't we just hate it? A great resume may get the job, but it won't ensure keeping it. Keeping the job will ensure your ability to eat, pay bills, and otherwise enjoy life. But you are not like that slacker described above, right? *Of course you aren't!*

Blank page for putting together summary sentences.

Blank page for putting together summary sentences.

Why Will I Be Good for a Company?
Summary Sentences From Your Personal Work Sheet

Questions You May Be Asked

16

Purpose of a Resume

The whole purpose of a resume is to *open the door for an interview*. An interview is a *face-to-face meeting* whereby another person determines whether or not you will *fit into their business*. What most ruins an interview is not thinking ahead of time about what they will want to know. Have someone ask you the following questions one at a time and you give an answer. Here are the questions.

1. Tell me about yourself.
2. Why are you on the job market?
3. What can you do for us?
4. What type of boss do you like?
5. What are your weaknesses?
6. What are your strengths?
7. What have you accomplished that is significant?
8. What salary do you want?

When you answered, were you hesitant? Did you act as if you had never thought of these things before? 'Duh' is not the best look you can have on your face during an interview. Granted, one cannot know everything an interviewer will ask, but it isn't as if the interview questions are unknown.

HINT!

If the question seems vague or could mean several different things, *do not hesitate to ask* what the question means. Asking for clarification or more information is a good trait and will be noted well. Stand in front of a mirror while you practice your answers. Do your eyes shift around? Are you relaxed or tense and uncomfortable?

Practice, practice, practice until the answers seem natural and automatic. Remember, 'duh' doesn't get the job.

1. **Tell me about yourself.**

In a concise, one- to two-minute reply, talk about your education, work experience, and how you will benefit the company.

HINT!

Do not lie or fudge the facts. Lies, distortions, and half-truths will come back to haunt you and it won't do your prospects any good. Yeah, yeah. Some people get away with it — *but not for long!*

Notes:

2. **Why are you in the job market?**

Simple, straight-forward answers work best. Be direct and quick. Do not hesitate longer than five or ten seconds. While pausing before answering, be sure to have a thoughtful look on your face. Remember, 'huh?' is not a good look to have on your face. Were you fired? Did you quit? Are you quitting? Why? Why? Why? Be honest.

HINT!

Please do not say "My boss hated me." You will come across as a cry-baby. No matter if it is the truth or not, leave personal feelings out of it. *No one cares!*

Notes:

3. What can you do for us?
This will necessitate knowing something about the company, its operations, and products or services.

HINT!

Go see your friendly public librarians. They can show you annual reports, company officers, percentage breakdown of product sales, who their main competitors are, gross annual sales, number of employees, even how much the company is in debt and how much cash they have in reserve. After you know some of this, then you are in a better position to know more specifically how you can help them.

Notes:

4. What type of boss do you like?
Do not make a joke (such as "the kind I never see.") Do not criticize your last boss ("no one likes my last boss; he is a jerk.") This question is often asked to throw you a curve. They want to see how you react under pressure. They do not really want to know what kind of boss you like. No, no, no. They really want to know what kind of worker you are.

HINT!

1. Will your boss have to hold your hand and lead you through every step of the process even after you have been trained?
2. Will your boss have to keep directing your attention to the task at hand?
3. Can you concentrate when things get hectic or are you easily distracted?
4. If your boss works closely with you, will you get upset and want to be left alone?
5. Do you work well with others and are you cooperative?

Notes:

5. What are your weaknesses?

Make a note about a failure you have had. Do not say you have no weaknesses or failures. Everyone does and has.

HINT!

> **Remember, too, that some weaknesses are just strengths used at the wrong time or too much. Make a note of one and how it affected past decisions, how you learned from it, and how you have worked on changing or modifying the strength.**

Notes on Failures:

Notes on Strengths disguised as Weaknesses:

6. What are your strengths?

Mention a strength and then give an example of how it has been used in a past position. Then do it again. Don't say you can do anything they need. No one can do everything. Besides, just how vague can you be? How desperate can you get? Also, do not say you can only do one thing (unless that thing is so stupendous and marvelous that it doesn't matter if you ever do anything else the rest of your life).

HINT!

> **In today's job market, everyone must be *versatile*, *adaptable* and *willing* to learn.**

Strength #1:

Strength #2:

Strength #3:

7. What have you accomplished that is significant?

Think about the last three years and list something for each year, if possible. What made you the proudest? Give numbers, if possible. Did you save the company money? How? Were you #1 in sales? Why?

HINT!

Interviewers need something concrete around which to form an opinion of you. It gives them a solid reason why their decision to hire you was good.

This Year:

Last Year:

The Previous Year:

---

8. What salary do you want?

Thinking positively about yourself and your abilities will help you avoid the tendency to ask for less than you are worth, which will probably mean you won't have to go out and get that second or third job. *Give a range* from lowest to highest with lowest establishing the least you can survive on.

HINT!

Yes, we all know you want as much as you can get, but that is a vague answer that really leaves the interviewer wondering if the company can afford you, or thinking you are a greedy so-and-so. It also shows a lack of knowledge about how business operates. *And again, just how vague can you get?*

Salary Requirements: *The least amount you can live on.*

Salary Requirements: *The highest your research shows this job will pay.*

Stress Interviews

This sort of interview doesn't happen all the time and you may never experience it. However, it is nice to know it exists. A stress interview is just what the name implies: *stressful*. It is extremely hard, even hostile and delivered in rapid fire fashion.

Its purpose? To see if you can take the heat. Since this is usually the last interview before hiring, if you experience this stress interview then you have already made several cuts. Congratulations. Remember, it isn't personal, it's just another test, so be prepared!

Note from Angela:

Marcia Champagne had a great thought about a bit of information she always likes to see on a resume. While it will not diminish your opportunities for interviews, as a headhunter—someone who is screening candidates—Marcia always find it extremely helpful if the candidate will tell her in one brief sentence what the company does because the name of the company does not always communicate its business type.

Examples of businesses that are clear:

BellSouth Mobility
Warner Brothers
Time Magazine
Blockbuster Video
McDonald's
The Original Mattress Factory

Examples of businesses that are NOT clear:

Associated Services
Ketchum and Ketchum
TRI
Ormandy
Lanier Worldwide, Inc.
Lason, Inc.
Gambrell & Stolz

Knowing the context within which you did your job gives the headhunter much more information with which to know you better. There are certain job types associated with each of these companies in the left column and they are clear because we know the type of business. But the right column is not so clear. Are they lawyers? Doctors? Accountants? Printers? Construction engineers? House movers? Stock brokers?

Resume #1: This is how most resumes look on paper.

DONALD H. "CHIP" JOHNSON
5187 Hackney Court
Granger, Indiana 99999
(404) 555-5555

OBJECTIVE: Position in sales or management of a company seeking to expand into a national market.

CAREER HISTORY:

A&B INDUSTRIES, INC.; ATLANTA, INDIANA
January 1991 - **SALES and MARKETING MANAGER**
Present:All-Do Industries, Inc. (404) - 555-5555
$3.2 million gross sales in 1992
Manufacturer of Industrial Towing Equipment.
›One of four managers directed by A&B Industries, Inc. to form new company.
›Designed **national** marketing and sales strategy to introduce new company to the industry, i.e., end users; foreign and domestic governments and municipalities.
›Sales; securing contracts; product field demonstrations.
›Established a national distributor network. Organized and directed company participation at national and international trade shows.

April 1989 - **SALES REPRESENTATIVE**
January 1991: ABC Wrecker Manufacturing.
$26 million gross sales in 1991.
›Established distributor network in four-state territory.

February 1987**TERMINAL MANAGER:** September 1988 to February 1989
March 1989:**ACCOUNT REPRESENTATIVE:** February 1987 to August 1988
On-the-Road Again Package System, Inc., Augusta, Georgia and Birmingham, Alabama
›Youngest Sales Manager ever promoted to Terminal Manager; after eighteen months. Responsible for daily operations
›Maintained terminal budgets; Conformed to stringent On-the-Road Again requirements; managed fifteen operations and sales personnel.
›Secured over new 100 accounts in fresh territory. Involved contacting managers and business owners and introducing them to the new transportation service.
›Regional winner of National Sales Contest two years in a row.

April 1985 -**SALES REPRESENTATIVE**
December 1986:Lower Forty-Eight Lines, Inc., Douglasville, Georgia
›Seven state territory with customer base ranging from Fortune 500 companies to small family operations.
›International overseas shipping of perishable and non-perishable products.

EDUCATION:

The University of Tennessee; Knoxville, Tennessee
Bachelor of Science
Major: Marketing
Graduated with Honors in 1984

References supplied upon request.

Resume #2: See comparison notes on next page.

DONALD H. "CHIP" JOHNSON

5187 Hackney Court
Granger, Indiana 99999
(404) 555-5555

OBJECTIVE:

Position in Sales or Management of a company seeking to expand into a national market.

- **QUALIFICATIONS**

Secured over 100 accounts in fresh territory.

Designed national marketing and sales strategy to introduce new company to the industry as well as foreign and domestic governments and municipalities.

Established a national distributor network.

- **CAREER HISTORY**

Sales And Marketing Manager
A&B Industries, Inc.; Atlanta, Indiana
January 1991 - Present:
$3.2 million gross sales in 1992. Manufacturer of Industrial Towing Equipment.
- One of four managers directed by A&B Industries, Inc., to form new company.

Sales Representative
ABC Wrecker Manufacturing; Atlanta, Indiana
April 1989 to January 1991
$26 million gross sales in 1991.
- Established distributor network in four-state territory.

Terminal Manager February 1987 to March 1989
Account Representative February 1987 to August 1988
On-the-Road Again Package System, Inc.,
Augusta, Georgia and Birmingham, Alabama
- Youngest Sales Manager ever promoted to Terminal Manager; after eighteen months.
- Responsible for daily operations.

Sales Representative
Lower Forty-Eight Lines, Inc., Douglasville, Georgia
April 1985 - December 1986
- Seven state territory with customer base ranging from Fortune 500 companies to small family operations.
- International overseas shipping of perishable and non-perishable products.

- **EDUCATION**

The University of Tennessee; Knoxville, Tennessee
Bachelor of Science
Major: Marketing
Graduated with Honors in 1984

PROFESSIONAL. FRIENDLY. QUALITY-MINDED.

PAY ATTENTION!
THIS IS IMPORTANT.

Resume readers spend a maximum of 30 seconds perusing each resume received. Resume #1, while listing impressive accomplishments, does little to highlight—or draw the eye toward—information most needed by the reader. Resume #2, on the other hand, spaces and breaks up information with the use of bullets, indentations, and bulleted indentations *plus* a judicious use of bold text.

Why isn't all the information of Resume #1 on Resume #2? That which was left out could just as easily be mentioned in a cover letter, but truly was not necessary to establish his credentials.

Notice the flow of the information. The *Objective* was very clear. The *Qualifications* list three major reasons, in order of importance, supporting his objective. The *Career History* lists most current (or most important) positions and companies. Again, these support the claim he is good at Sales and Management. If during this period he worked at a fast-food establishment simply asking 'you want fries with that', well, it would just be best to leave that out since it would only serve to detract from his qualifications.

Education comes next. See the Education Section for these tips. *Skills Summary* was not included on this resume. I feel it was a mistake; he could have listed industry specific software programs with which he was familiar, etc. However, he did not and he was the customer. On the other hand, when you list the summary of your skills, please remember to group them in order of importance to your job objective OR how well you perform them.

Notice the bottom of the Resume #2 page. Donald has listed three traits he feels accurately sums up his work ethic and business mind. This listing has been questioned on more than one occasion by professional resume preparers. However, I have received too many favorable phone calls to leave it off. My customers have related stories about the positive impact the three trait summation had on an interviewer. One interviewer commented the three traits "are what motivated me to set up an interview". You will get these three words from the list in the section called *Describe Yourself*.

PAY ATTENTION! THIS IS THE CHECKLIST FOR YOUR RESUME.

1. Spelling.

2. Current address and phone numbers, even E-Mail.

3. Margins (not to narrow and not too wide).

4. Tabs (evenly spaced horizontally).

5. Bullets (not HUGE or too many).

6. Spacing (not crowded!).

Want a RAISE that is more than the typical cost of living raise?

Listen, there is nothing guaranteed in this world. But one thing is for sure—if you go to your employer telling them you NEED a raise because of something going on in your life, the employer is almost sure to say no, forget it, and stop whining. You like the job, you like the people you work with, you even like the people you work for, but you really do want that raise. So what do you do?

You think like a business owner! A business owner incurs fixed and variable costs to service his customers. In order to keep his doors open he must charge his customers enough to cover all those costs plus enough to save for the future when business is slow (it happens to all businesses) while costs remain the same (you still want your paycheck, right?) Therefore, any increase in those costs seriously impacts on his ability to meet payroll, etc.

Before the business owner increases those costs, he looks to see if the benefit of the services outweighs the price he is paying. This is called a cost/benefit analysis. At this point he is paying you a set salary. That is how much your services are worth to him. Why should he pay more?

Ah! This is where the **Career Information Manager and Interview Preparation Guide** portion of this book comes in handy. Remember, it is all about tooting your own horn; letting your light shine; advertising you. Go through this section. Write everything you can think of that you have been doing for your employer that either:

1. Saves them money.
2. Saves them time (which, by the way, is money).
3. Makes them money.
4. Or in some other way really contributes to the financial health of that business.
5. That wasn't done before you got there.
6. That is only done by you.

Put together a resume as it applies to the meeting you will have. Prepare two copies, one for you, one for him. Then ask for an appointment; 30 minutes should do it. Don't say why. When you get to the meeting, do not use the words *"I NEED a raise"*. Why not? Because your needs have nothing to do with the employer's needs.

Instead, tell him you would like to review what you do for the company and how much the company benefits. Go over the points on the paper and give examples and amounts, if possible. At the end tell him you believe the value you have added to his company more than justifies a small increase in salary.

Then tell him how much you want. The amount you ask for is such a variable that I really couldn't comment on it here, but remember, if it isn't reasonable the discussion will end. And, unless you have a legitimate, for real, job offer from another source, don't threaten to quit. A decent paycheck is better than no paycheck at all.

There is a saying in sales: a no answer is simply a request for more information. Help your employer justify the added cost of employing you. Plus, other employees will find out about your raise. (You KNOW they will.) They will want one, too. Help your boss make his decision look like a sound business move instead of a favor done for the teacher's pet.

If the answer is still no, you find the situation untenable and really must have more money, then use this book to prepare a killer resume and begin your job hunt. After all, you now have proof of your worth. Later, should you get a better job offer and your employer really wants to keep you, he may decide to offer you more.

Either way, you are in control as much as it is possible to be. That is a good feeling.

Feeling ignored when you send out your resume?

Then get attention by making sure your advertisement stands head and shoulders above the crowd. This book is based on client consultations conducted since 1992. It guides you through the self-advertising process and even helps you make a great paper presentation. Make a copy of this page. Order extra copies for your friends and relatives as gifts. Recommend it to your workmates. Remember—order 2 or more at one time and the price only gets better.

1. Order this book from your favorite bookstore or

2. Call Toll Free: 1 (800) 431-1579 to order with

3. Or send a check or money order made payable to the publisher at:

> **WRITER for HIRE!**
> **648 McKenzie Circle**
> **Stockbridge, GA 30281**   **Email comments welcome:**
> **(770) 389-4321**   **Angelawrtr4hre@msn.com**

PS: Payments by money order to publisher are shipped the following day.
Payments by check to publisher are shipped after the check clears.

Name: _____

Address: _____

_____

Apt./Suite: _____

City: _____

State: ____ ZIP: _____

Daytime Phone: (____) _____

Evening Phone: (____) _____

Fax: (____) _____

Email Address:

_____

Please send me *Nine Stupid Things People Do To Mess Up Their Resume.*

Copies		Price	Total
☐ 1	@	$11.95	_____
☐ 2-5	@	$9.95 ea.	_____
☐ 6-10	@	$8.95 ea	_____

Need More? Call for Bulk Pricing.

Subtotal: $_____

GA. Tax 7%   _____

Shipping:
1	@	$4.00	_____
2-5	@	$6.50	
6-10	@	$12.50	_____

TOTAL $_____

Thank you so much for your purchase. Each time my book is purchased, it allows me to give another lesson to my children in the workings and benefits of the free-marketplace.
Sincerely, Angela K. Durden — Author (and Wife, Mom, Business Owner, and Publisher!)